Apologies Hypocrisy/ A Lyrical Year

Tom Clement

chipmunkapublishing
the mental health publisher

Published by
Chipmunkapublishing
United Kingdom

http://www.chipmunkapublishing.com

ISBN   978-1-78382-138-9

Chipmunkapublishing gratefully acknowledge the support of Arts Council England.

The Background...

During an unstable childhood, Tom's mental health began to wane and, after two members of his family committed suicide, Tom found himself sectioned under The Mental Health Act, at just sixteen years of age, experiencing an intense psychosis that lasted several years.

During his time in hospital, Tom found solace in music and wrote lyrics to pass his time and help focus away from the world he was living in. The majority of those lyrics written during his time in hospital are presented to you in this book. Now in recovery from his illness, Tom still likes to express himself through rhyme and lyric, with newer works included in this book sharing a broader understanding of his journey.

Tom Clement

Apology's Hypocrisy

These lyrics show a side of me that's different to the lyrics that are in my biography and lets you know some of the feelings I had while writing my biography 'What Will Other People Think' that I didn't want to include in the book. My biography needed to end on the right note and these lyrics didn't fit.

This project shed's some more light on where I've been and hints at where I hope to be going. You don't need to read my biography to follow this, but you might gain a better understanding of where these lyrics are coming from. My biography is titled 'What Will Other People Think?' and is also available at www.chipmunkapublishing.co.uk

What's the difference between poetry and lyric writing? I have been asked before, why don't I call my work poems instead of lyrics? While poetry is allowed to flow freely and take on what structure, or lack of structure, it chooses, lyrics have more emphasis on the syllable structure and rhyming pattern. Like old folk ballads, the focus is on keeping words that rhyme within its rhythmic structure.

'An Apology' was written when I was feeling quite angry about my time in the psychiatric ward and how those of us in the system are looked down on. It's partly my biography lyric and partly a campaign song.

'Should Have Known' is to someone who features in the last few chapters of my biography. It was written as an attempt to make sense of Janet Jackson's 'Velvet Rope', while being motivated by listening to Mariah Carey's 'Side Effects',

'Shame' is a little ditty I wrote for a song contest. It's a bit of a 'Prince: Sign Of The Times' lyric, while the lyric 'Don't You Want To See' shares how I feel about some of today's social discomfort.. I also try to sensitively approach the topic of self-harm in the lyric 'Don't Bleed'.

I've also included three lyrics I wrote for other peoples instrumentals on a couple of music courses. I've noticed that my approach to writing for other peoples instrumentals is simpler, but more fluid and relaxed. 'I Won't Say It' is one or the lyrics written. I wrote it quite quickly to fit a student's instrumental, but I believe in the lyrics I wrote and hope to get it recorded one day.

Tom Clement

All work and sayings in this book are my own.

I haven't lost my marbles, I've got too many

An Apology

V1:

I never made it to college cos during the holiday
Society decided I was mad and threw me away
Cutting me off from all my family and friends
My best friend must have thought I was dead
He never saw me again

Locked up under section 2, it goes on your record
I wasn't a criminal but still I was scorned
I was kept on the ward
Couldn't close any doors
As if I didn't already feel insecure
Followed through the hall
They noted every mouthful
Couldn't work out if the nurses wanted to help
Or just wanted to be cruel

8 months later I was spat out and told to cope
And then frowned upon cos I wasn't in work

Chorus:

Well, this is me
This is me, this is me, this is me
And if you want an apology you can stuff it
I can't stomach the injustice cast upon us
By the judgement of the loveless
Have you tried living with voices telling you to die?
Have you battled a void that's trying to claim your life?
You want me to work with all the **** in my head?
Aren't you surprised I'm not already dead?
Well I've got news for you, I'm not going nowhere
My only career is trying to make you care
Not about me but about your family and friends
Don't you know one in four of us face lonely despair?
Maybe it's not me but society
That should be offering an apology

V2:

I had a good psychiatrist and CPN
But the government decided to take money from them
So now I have to wait longer to see them again
Cos the mentally ill aren't worth nothing to the NHS

I'd prefer to get well, have a job, love and kids
Than spend my life struggling on benefit
But once you're labelled
You're deemed wasteful
It's disgraceful
People attitudes are shameful
My life's been disabled
But people are hateful

How would you feel if this happened to you?
Don't you think it's about time that a change is due?

Bridge:

Don't talk about it be about it
Don't talk about it be about it
Don't talk about it be about it
Ain't that right Mos Def
Are you hearing me yet?

Don't talk about it be about it
Don't talk about it be about it
Don't talk about it be about it
Are you feeling me yet?
Did you hear what I said?

Ending:

Don't you think it's about time
That a change is due?
How would you feel
If this happened to you?

Don't you think it's about time
That a change is due?
How would you feel
If this happened to you?

To the winds
© *T.Clement 08*

Should Have Known

V1:

I was fresh from a war
You needed something to hold on to
I was feeling insecure
But you knew that didn't you
I thought that I knew a stranger
But I couldn't see the dangers
I was blinded by your eyes
Wish I could have seen inside

The words were new to me
But you'd used them times before
I thought you were sincere
But you played me like a fool
And a part of me knew it
But I thought this time was different
But just like every mistake
I didn't realise till too late

Chorus:

I guess I should have known better
Than to let you near
You gave my heart your velvet rope
And strangled my soul with it
I should have known you couldn't be trusted
I should have known you never really cared
I should have known I was convenient
I should have known to be prepared

V2:

You said I would succeed
With you by my side
But then you trampled on my dreams
And told me to leave them behind
You sold me your vision
But it became my prison
But I was denial
I couldn't accept the signs

Those who knew you said beware
That you're all you were about
I thought they weren't being fair
But the truth stands clearly now
You put out the fire in my heart
And let it cinder in the dark
You extinguished every flame
Because you had to have your way

Bridge:

So you had it your way
Again and again
I neglected my friends
Because you knew best
And you watched me wilt
After everything I'd built
You just turned your head
After you got what you needed

I should have known to trust my soul
I should have known that you had to go
I should have seen you take control
I should have never stayed so long…

To the weeds
© *T.Clement 08*

Shame

V1:

Now you think that you know me
But you don't know me
You only
Think I'm that guy on the corner
You think I'm shady, I'll rob you.
You hear me walking behind you
You even think I might knife you
You don't really want to know me
'Cos you're already my jury

You think that you've got to be wary
Of someone that's as sane as me
Cos to be sane is crazy
In this world today

Chorus:

Ain't that a shame
The only way
You can feel safe
Is when you say
That you're the only one
You can count on.....
What's with this place
It's such a state
Everyone claims
There's only hate
Left in today's young ones
Yet I still feel love.....

V2:

Kids stuck on their sofas
Cos they're scared they'll be run over
Or get caught in a drive by
If they venture outside.
Mum and Dad are so cautious
That their kids are unsure if
The world's really their oyster
Cos there is no choice anymore

Something like that happened to me
I grew too afraid to be free
But if you resign yourself to defeat
Then you'll never break your chains

Bridge:

There's more colours than black and white
There're more options than wrong and right
There's more to us than hate and blame
Can't you believe we're all the same?

To how it is
© *T.Clement 07*

13

Forgotten

I don't want to go home

And be left by myself.

My neighbours take others in

And leave me alone

Where I cry

Listening to their laughter on the other side.

I'm never part of it

Or maybe I am

They all talk about me here

I talk to them and they talk about me

But not to me.

I yelled with all my being once

Just to see if anyone noticed or cared

Like I did when I heard someone shout

And went to see if they were ok.

Nobody came to see if I was ok.

They didn't talk to me for months actually

Even though I said hi.

I was here first

And introduced them all

And now I'm forgotten.

To 2011

Put Down Your Pride

V1:

In your purple haze
You were encouraged to misread the signs
And made a mistake.
Humiliated me in front of other eyes
And through a good thing away.
And I halted in disbelief
At what you thought was true about me
It's not like you to get things wrong
But you should have known me better.

So now you realise that you got it wrong
But you're too proud to be humble
I'm easy to talk to, you should know
But you've prefer to keep this burning

Chorus:

Can't you accept that you made a mistake
Isn't friendship worth more than hate
I know you won't say sorry
I know you won't apologize
But you don't have to say those words to put things right
Just put down your pride.

V2:

It wasn't your fault
It wasn't mine
But how you've been to me since
Cuts like a knife
You know it's criminal
To treat people this way
And it's all been to spare your pride.

But you know I stand my ground
And if I'm not wrong I don't back down
So talking behind my back I won't allow.
You can keep firing blanks
All day long
But you've got nothing on me
And still I'm willing to talk

I'm willing to get back on track
But you think you can't do that
Cos you're too proud to go back on your word
Even though you know it has no worth.

Bridge:

To protect yourself you've spread your words
To play the blame game
You thought you could play chess with me
But this is stale mate
And the only reason you're not checked
Is cos I've still got some respect for you
Some respect for us.

Have you heard that pride comes
Before a fall
I want to pick us up
But you would rather crawl.
Sometimes I wish I did something wrong
So that I could say sorry and put this right
I wonder if you ever look at me
And ask if this was all worth while

To what it's worth
© T.Clement '12

Don't You Want To See

V1

I don't understand
That look in your eyes
An anger you have
Over what you feel's been denied
Not being treated
Like everyone else
But you need to respect others
If you want that for yourself

What motivates you
To think like you do?
It's not that you want more
Than other people
It's that you want other people
To have less than you

Every action has a reaction
So what will that be?
How will that effect
Your community?

Chorus:

Don't you want to be a better man
Don't you want to see a better land
There's a better future to be had
If you want to be a better man

V2

There ain't no excuses
For what you've been doing
You say that when you were young
You saw your mum get beaten
Did you think that that's how
You should treat them?
Did it make you smile
To see her cry?
Did you think that's what
You want in life?

At the moment of your birth
Your mum knew your worth
And wanted you to be part
Of a better world
Not causing hurt
And making things worse
But to be part of something better
People need to come together

So conduct yourself
In the correct code
And make your town see
That up you've grown

Bridge:

Weed breeds apathy
Or seeds greed vindictively
Wanting more than you are owed
Paranoid you'll lose your thrown
You are what you eat
So stop feasting on fear
Don't feed a child lies
And poison their mind

It's up to you to choose
Your destiny
And not let others choose
Who you need to be
And not let others
Fill you with hate
Or Lead you astray
Or decide your fate
Don't demonise
The hands that bind
Or seek divide
Causing suspicious eyes

Wires get crossed
Lost in translation
We want unison
Not separation
Let's speak the same language
So that we're on the same page
Make black words
On white paper
Easier to translate

Don't you want to see a better land
Don't you want to make a better plan
There's a better future to be had
If you want to see a better land

To betterness
© *T.Clement '14*

#*sickworld*

Little boy bullied with bruises
Despairing youth, he ties the noose
And steps off the chair
Unable to see a future through

And on facebook they laugh
Their victory has been had
His bullies have succeeded
In breaking a spirit

#sickworld

Kids thinking it's fun to terrorize
A woman walking alone at night
Talking abuse while laughing at her
Thinking it's fun to snatch the bag off her

#sickworld

Terrorists behead kids fathers
Uploading proof on the internet
Allowing their children to replay
Their fathers death

#sickworld

Planes shot down deliberately
Passengers' bodies hidden from family
Loved ones never laid to rest in peace

#sickworld

Government greed
Votes to legalise weed
Let the kids smoke the reef
Watch their brain cells deplete
End up hospitalised
On wards there for psychiatry

#sickworld

Don't Bleed

V1

It's just crossed your mind again
I'm not oblivious
I know you're minds in pain
And I've seen the switch flick behind your eyes.

You go to the bathroom
The door locks there
Keep love out of that room.
You feel life's unjust
And you've been used
They did wrong to you
So you do wrong to you too

Chorus

But two wrongs don't make things right
And pain plus pain doesn't ease the mind
I know the knife cuts so easily
But don't bleed
Don't bleed

V2:

You bare war wounds
Of a tortured soul
Wear them with pride
To show you've survived.
But you don't want to score
Another home goal
You're worth more than the lies
That repeat in your mind

Bridge:

True friends don't want you
To cause yourself pain
There's no unity in mutilation
Don't let twits
Tell you what to do
You don't need their evaluation.
Sometimes you take weed to numb the pain
And then bleed to feel alive again
It's ok to wear your heart on your sleeve
But don't bleed
Don't bleed

Loneliness
Distress
It's so intense
Everything inside
You want to express.
You can't rest
Each breath
Feels like more life spent
But you won't break
Because you've got the strength.

The tension that burns under your skin
The intensity of what's within
Can subside if you realign your mind
Exhale, inhale
Breath in new life

Cos two wrongs don't make things right
And pain plus pain doesn't ease the mind
I know the knife cuts so easily
But don't bleed
Don't bleed.

To those who struggle
© *T.Clement '14*

My Favourite Sin

V1:

I know you're heartless
But tonight you're dressed to kill
And I might be your victim
If I have my way
We never lasted
But you haunt me still
And tonight you can possess me
Let's reignite our flame

Chorus:

Because don't you know
You're my favourite sin
And we can do anything
Tonight
I'm sure you know
You're my favourite sin
And we can do anything
Tonight

V2:

Somewhere in this darkness
I'll find my delight
And all that you'll be to me
Is a satisfying night
Forget how we parted
It doesn't matter anymore
I've got all you need right here
So what are you waiting for

Hook:

I know love hurts
And babe you're the worst
But my fire burns
For you tonight

© *T.Clement '09*

Want Something True

V1

For too many night now
Have I tossed and turned restlessly
While I watch you lie
Sleeping peacefully in our bed
Wish I could dream
That we were in love again
But we both see the truth now
And I cannot pretend

Chorus

Oh
We both can't live like this
When our love is gone
What we got
Is no longer worth fighting for
Oh
I'm hurting right here
So I'll pack up and go
I deserve
Much better
And I want something true

V2

I'll pack up my things
While you see who you dream of
Because we both know that our love
Won't wake up again
I've tried to put right
The wrongs that we were both making
But you think it's alright
To live like we're strangers
And forget that we once were friends

Oh
We both can't live like this
When our love is gone
What we've got
Is no longer worth fighting for
Oh
I'm hurting right here
S I'll pack up and go
I deserve
Much better
And I want something true

I Won't Say It

V1:

And when I found you babe
It was you who made me change
People never thought I'd
Come around to seeing a better way

You did it babe
You saw potential in me

It hasn't been that long
But you've really got
Under my veins
You've made me realise
That I can still change my
Negative ways

It's not too late
Life's just begun with you
Thought I'd never relate (to them)
But you're helping me change
My point of view

Chorus:

I won't say it
But I think I'm falling in love with you babe

Every day
You make me find more reasons why
I want to be with you

V2:

I've not been here before
I've never found something
So warm
My hearts been beaten black and blue
But now it sees
The colour of you

But I can't let it show
Can't let everyone know
That's not the way I work
But still this feelings grown

Chorus:

I won't say it
But I think I'm falling in love with you babe

Every day
You make me find more reasons why
I want to be with you.

© T.Clement '10

Even horses can have an identity crisis

Peace.

Current Projects

I've recently discovered the world of street art character design and the Urban Vinyl movement, which has rejuvenated some of my love for creating.

In 2010 I entered into a worldwide character toy design contest and made it to the final hundred. Only myself and one other designer from the UK made it to the final hundred!

My design was created and went on show in a gallery in Asia where the contest was held.
Here's my entry and gallery piece below:

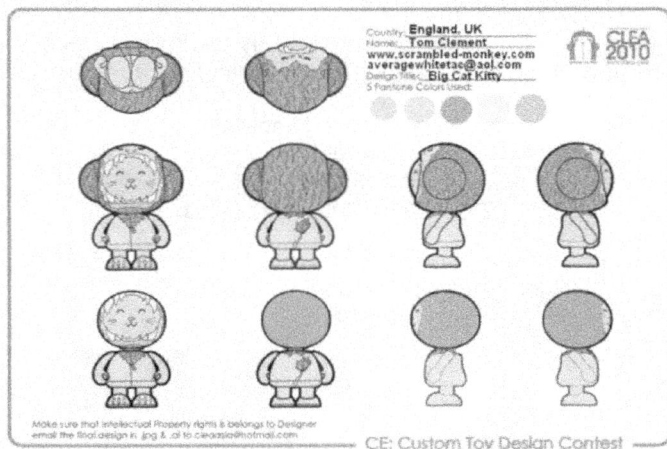

My design in the gallery, along with my 'certificate', the little dude on the right saying I made it to the final hundred :o)

This will be an ongoing interest and I now have a website for my creative junk
Here, called:
www.scrambledmonkey.co.uk

You can also find a design album on public view on my Facebook page: www.facebook.com/scrambledmonkey
:o)

Just one more . .

**It means nothing more
than everything**

Oh my god I love her
There'll never be another
You only get one mother
And I can't bear to see her suffer.
I just want to hug her
And I hope she sees some summers
I say we'll see some wonders
At the Olympics in London.
You're with us now Mum and that's what matters
We'll get back on track before things get blacker
We'll attack this from all angles
So don't give up Mum, that's not allowed now.

I believe in you Mum.

©2009

...and just another one more..

You Taught Me The Word

I wish we knew what to say
Without letting every day
Slip away
Cos these are precious times together
I wish you'd say how you felt
We should be free to be ourselves
Life is about sharing
It's unfair if we live like strangers

I regret we're not as close
As my soul wants us to be
Maybe a part is down to you
But most is down to me
I'm scared to hold on to something
That I know I could well loose
But I might never really love
If I don't tell you the truth

We are only human
And don't always know the best route to take
But the pains of yesterday
Are not as inviting as your embrace today
I know that fate could not be seen
But you've always wanted the best for me

I know it's not been easy
The greatest journeys never are
But it would amount to nothing
If I don't say what's in my heart

This Journey into the unknown
Has helped both of us grow
But we both want something better
And I hope we find it together
We've stood side by side
While others have gone their separate ways
Because somewhere inside of us
We've always kept the faith

You taught me the word

Love

You showed me the word

Love

I might never have known

Love

If it wasn't for you

To Mum, Dad and family
© Jan 2008, T.Clement

You cannot encourage a tree to grow
By cutting it roots

Mountains may crumble,
But you can get up again.

Tom Clement

A Lyrical Year

I had this idea which crossed my mind during the writing of my biography. What you have here in 'A Lyrical Year' are a selection of some of the very first poems, rhymes and lyrics I ever wrote. Most of them were written during the time I spent in the psychiatric ward, mostly as a way of escapism, to alleviate boredom, or to express things I couldn't say.

Most of these were written when I was 16, and a couple when I was 17. This was also during the time when acts such as Steps and Billie Piper were topping the charts, whose songs I saw as my competitors! Because of that, I don't see the melodies I had for these songs as being relevant anymore. But you might still find something in the lyrics.

While reading these lyrics you might want to ask yourself the same question I did while I was typing them up. I was sectioned under the mental health act because I was seen to be a risk to myself or others. The question to ask yourself here is: Do the words expressed here really show a mind so unstable that they need to be sectioned?

I'll let you think about that..

Poem

Bee's buzzing
In the springtime bloom
Sun shining
Banishing the gloom
Birds chirping
Amongst the coloured trees
Butterflies flutter
In the springtime breeze
Freedoms what matters let the animals rejoice
Human arrogance grows fatter
Deaf to nature's voice

Poem

Love hope and faith
Don't live without them
Don't make them go away
Or you'll die without them
Be happy every day
Week month and year
Love hope and faith
Don't make them disappear

Poem

The Lord he shines above us
Each and every day
And whenever we are troubled
He's willing to show us the way
If we just open our hearts to him
Let him into our lives
He's willing to shelter us
And make our spirits wise

The Lord he'll always love us
Forgive us of sin
We just need to open up our hearts
And put our trust in him

Poem

Leap Year Girl

You're twenty, but you're four
When you're sixty, you'll be fifteen
You're forever young little leap year girl
And that's how you want it to be
But when you are sixty
Will you be doing your GCSE's?
If you're forever young little leap year girl
How can you make life what you want it to be?

Lonely Tonight

V1:

I watch the dawn rise
I hear the cockerel crow
And then I realise
Without you I'm alone
I get up every morning
Begin each new day
But so many things
They just get in the way
And I break down and cry
Because I don't want to live
Without you

Chorus:

I'm gonna be lonely tonight
And you know that I won't feel right
Gonna be lonely tonight
Because you're not here
Not here by my side

V2:

I arrive at school late
Because you're on my mind
I can't seem to do anything
Since you've left my life
My friends are getting angry
Say you weren't't for me
But they'll never know
The way I loved you so
And they'll never know
The way you showed your love to me

Bridge:

I can be strong
Get through this alright
Even if it means that I'm
Lonely tonight
I know that I am strong
I know I can succeed
I know I can do anything
I know that I don't need you to need me
I know that I won't breakdown
If you're with some other guy and not me
But I still I know

Chorus:

I'm gonna be lonely tonight
And you know that I won't feel right
Gonna be lonely tonight
Because you're not here
Not here by my side
And even if I could put it right
How long will it be till we fight
How long would you be by my side
Lonely tonight
So lonely tonight

Poem

Sometimes at night
I look at the sky
And ask the world
Can you answer me tonight
Dear Lord I need to know
If everything will be alright
You know I've got so much on my mind
And it's tearing me up inside

Friends

Intro:

Friendship
Is what everyone needs
We all need someone to turn to
When we are in need
Sometimes
When we're feeling down
It helps if we have someone around
To light up our faces
And show us the road we should take

Friends should stand by through thick and thin
Friends will always be there till the end
Friends will be around for eternity
That's all you need to get by
That's why

Chorus:

You can count on your friends to be there
You can count on your friends when you need them
You can count on your friends when you're falling down
There'll always be someone around

V1:

When you do need someone
To help you get through
You can always count on me
I know I can count on you
You should help each other
Get through each new day
Don't let yesterday's worries
Get in today's way

We help each other
Travel through life's journey
If we come to a bend
We'll tell each other 'don't you worry'

V2:

I'll always be there till
The very last day
And we say goodbye
Our friendship will never go away
It's time to celebrate the
Bond that we have
I'll live my life in good will
No point not living like that

When you have good
Friends like these
There's no time for
Any enemies

Bridge:

Every now and then
We need a shoulder to cry on
We all need someone
That we know we can rely on
To be there
To show us the light that's through the tunnel
To support us
To give us hope and show us the way

Poem

While I was waiting
Lord I prayed
I prayed for that special day
While I was waiting
Lord I praised
I praised you for loving me in that special way
While I was waiting
I thought of my love
Thought of my love for you and your son
While I was waiting
I knew I'd be blessed
Blessed for when that special day would come
Now I don't have to wait much longer
Loving you has made me stronger
I know that day is soon to come
I know what I've prayed for will soon be done
I love you Lord

Please Don't Tell Me

Chorus:

Please don't tell me
What to do
I know you love me
And I love you
But right now I just need to be
Left alone
I'll sort it out on my own
Please don't tell me
What you think I should do

V1:

I'm all alone
Sitting here right now
I know it's sad
But I know that it's allowed
I need my space
Why can't you understand
Why can't you go away
Why can't you let me be my own man
I'm not awkward
I just need time to think
About what I'm doing
So please don't make me sink

V2:

I'm growing up now
So please don't push me down
I'm not a little kid anymore
I'm not acting a clown
So please don't push me around
Until I really know what it's for
Can't you be rational
You say you've been through it yourself
But then you'd understand
I'd come to you
When I need help
But that ain't now

Bridge:

Please don't be so mean to me
I'm only trying to follow my destiny
Just because you killed your dream
Doesn't mean you have to do the same to me
We can live together
In harmony
If you just allow me
To be me
I love you
You love me
But I really need you
To understand
What I mean
When I say
Go away

Poems about the Section:

How can you be patient
In a world of inpatients
You want to believe
In a world of disbelief
How come you're forced to do something
In a 'pressure free' environment
Stop the lying
While I'm here I'm dying
Mind and soul clinging
To the love of God
I'm not letting go
Just because they don't believe
Doesn't mean it ain't so

Loneliness is spreading in
Mind and soul diminishing
But my faith in God
Stands tall and strong
And I pray to him
All night long
My belief is stronger
Than anything
My love for God
Will make me win
If having faith is a crime
Then I am guilty
But remember who you pray to
In your time of need

Why am I here?
Under section 2?
What exactly did I do?
Why do you want to put me through
All this pain and suffering?
I've done nothing wrong!
Given my heart to one song
Let my belief in the Lord grow strong
In order to carry on
There is nothing you can do for me
Under section 2 you see
The Lord tells us to wait patiently
Open you heart
Then you'll see

Can I go home this weekend?
Why not?
I've done nothing wrong!
I am no threat
To myself or anyone
I've been put here for unjust reasons
And I refuse to watch all seasons
Pass me by
In this pig sty
I would rather die
Than be confined

Poem

The deed has been done
Am I set free?
No Lord, not yet
But soon I will be
Free to live, to laugh, to play
Free to work, do things my way
Free to win, to lose, to draw
Free to do right, knowing what for
I baptize myself
In this water unclean
And I wait patiently
For this summer's eve
Knowing my Lord that soon I'll be free
Because Lord my dear Lord
For your love for me
The deed has been done
Am I set free?
No Lord, not yet
But soon I will be

Hey High Flyer

Chorus:

Hey high flyer
Come down to me
Let me help give you
The love you seek
I admire that you fly
But you'll never reach the sky
If you don't have love
Deep in your life
Hey high flyer
Don't be ashamed
Be like a lion
That has no need to be tamed
Hey high flyer
Come down to me
Let me help give you
The love that you need.

V1:

Don't be afraid
To fall to the ground
When love is guiding your way
You'll rarely become down
Let love light up your life
In every corner of your heart
The hardest question you'll face
Is where exactly do I start?

I have been through all of this before
Let me tell you exactly
What's in store
Promise me you won't be afraid
Aim yourself
Towards your goal

V2:

You can never
Aim yourself too high
Although some of your friends
Will ask themselves why
Tell them they don't need to worry
But thanks for the thoughts
But you will try to make your own way
Without any pause

Reach for the sky
Don't ever stop
Just keep on trying
Till you're at the top
Follow your dream
But even if you fall
You'll get exactly what you need
And the Lord will answer your call

Bridge:

Just be patient
Dreams take a little time
But when you get there
You can never go too high
That's why
You have to try

Please Listen To Me

Chorus:

Please listen to me
I'll get you through it
There ain't nothing we can't do
If I'm with you
Please listen to me
I'll take you to it
Right to the top
We'll never stop

V1:

Please listen to me
Hear me out loud
Listen to the music
To push away the rainy clouds
When we're together
In body or in mind
We'll start fighting
Make the badness fall behind

With you
When I'm with you
I'll get you through
All the rainy days
I'll help you find
Your piece of mind
Don't wait for the right time
Just begin the fight

V2:

You are my best friend
I'll always be there for you
Never reach the end [of your tether]
Just keep it cool like you do
I'll help you get through
All the rainy days
We'll push the dark clouds away
For a brand new sunny day
A new time to begin
Keep on fighting like you do

With you
When I'm with you
I'll get you through
All the rainy days
I'll help you find
Your piece of mind
Don't wait for the right time
Just begin the fight

Bridge:

Never stop
Never drop
Pick yourself up off the floor
Don't be blind
Don't fall behind
Because you're capable
Of so much more

Keep Faith

Sept '98

Chorus:

Keep faith
To light the way
Step out of the night
And into the day
Don't put yourself down
Sort yourself out
The sun always shines
After the rain
Allow yourself love
Sort out the bad stuff
At the end of the day
There's always a way

V1:

When you're feeling down
Turn yourself around
Put on a happy face
Get rid of that frown
You can light up each day
In so many different ways
Keep yourself motivated
Don't turn in to clay

V2:

If you want a wish come true
Especially for you
Keep working hard at it
Don't give in to the blues
Throw out yesterday's troubles
Put them all away
And remember that tomorrow
Is the start of a brand new day

Bridge:

I want you to promise me that you'll work it out
And remember that happiness
For every person is allowed
Don't give up
Use your stuff
Don't be rough
Give in to love

Don't Be Scared

Chorus:

Don't be scared
I know you're going unprepared
But your dreams right there
Guiding you

V1:

I used to go on
Without a song in my heart
But I used to be happy
When I should have fallen apart
You see, when you're blind
You can't fall behind
Because you can't see the finish line
..Nor can you see the start
Yes I had to
Go through the blues
But eventually
I did get used to it
Don't worry
Love will be there soon
Hold on
Be strong
Please carry on

V2:

When I went through the tough times
I used to look back
To when I was happy
But the past was full of lies
Because it was not me
Just a manifestation
Of what people made me to be
But now
After I've strolled through the rain
And have seen
The sun shine again
I believe
That if this path was not conceived
I wouldn't be here today
I would have definitely lost my way

Bridge:

No one lives all their life
Without misery
So you see nothing's complete
Till all the colours have been received
But through it all
First and foremost
Have faith and believe
Never end your dream

This is what they mean
When they say
The Lord God above
Works in mysterious ways
Remember he sent the rain
Be patient with the rain
In time it will go away
And you'll see the sun again

Just Call My Name

Chorus:

Just call my name
And I'll be right there
Mother and father
You know that I care
There'll always be
Plenty of love to spare
So don't worry
I'll be right there

V1:

I love you Mother
With all my heart and soul
I love you Father
You just let me know
When you need me
I'll make sure I'm free
And I'll be right there for you
Don't worry
I'll never be too busy to call you
And make sure you're alright
If you need me to hold tight
I'll be right there
I said I'll be right there
Just call my name

We've been through a lot
In the life time that I've known you
And Lord knows I care
Because as my parents
You were always there for me
To bathe my wounds
And I will always be
Eternally grateful
For all you've given me
Love and health
Be it short of wealth
But I am here
To repay you now

V2:

I may not have got what I wanted
And you couldn't give me just what I needed
But you always cared for me
I know times were hard
And you let down your guard
But there'll always be
Love for you inside of me
Through your mistakes I learned
Couldn't have been here if it weren't for you
And your mistakes you put me through
I'm grateful I tasted the hardship
Before I tasted the sweetness
You gave me a chance to learn
You taught me to work hard to earn
I'll always love you
And I'll always give you
The love you need

Bridge:

You're only human
And a human makes mistakes
When I needed time for my dream
I understand
Why you thought you couldn't wait
I understand
That you thought it'd be too late
Although you gave me pressure
For no reason
I'll love you forever
Through each and every season
Just call my name

Dear Lord

Chorus:

Dear Lord
Please Lord
Please help me if you can
I know that I'm a man
But I can't change the world
And if
You knew
Everything that's going on
Can you right the wrongs
That we've made

V1:

I was alone
With no friend in the world
I cried so many things of shame
But was never
Heard
Until my Lord
I learnt of your love
That was enough to make me begin

You hatched my egg
And out I came
A brand new me
That carried no shame
Knew what I must gain
What things must be obtained
From life's game

Now I pray
For the other sake
Who know no love
But only hate
I know they'll die
If they stay this way
Please Lord, dear Lord
Help them for their sake

V2:

How can we help
Turn the world around
We've got to help ourselves
Before we all fall down
Why can't it just be
Goodness that's allowed
How does the badness
Find its way back round

We try so hard to make things right
But is peace truly
Out of our sight
No
Because it's in our minds lord I pray
Every night

Bridge:

Why do we hate
Each other so bad
When I think about it
It makes me so sad
Lord, dear Lord
Why can't we just be glad
For all the possessions
That we have

Why do we care
So much about wealth
When all we really need
Is goodness and health
Where is the love
When there is no trust
To turn ourselves around
Before we all break down

First True Love

Chorus:

You were my first true love
Allowed inside my heart
But I'll never forget the day
My heart got torn apart
We should have made our way through it
'Cause there was nothing to it
We could have got by
With a little time

V1:

The day I asked you out
Felt like the best day of my life
I never felt so alive and free
That time felt so right
But how was I to know
That I was your bit on the side
I thought we'd be together for life

V2:

The first night I loved you
Was the day before I knew
The earth definitely moved
When I was there with you
But how was I to know
That you led another life
Where you thought it would be alright
To tell me your loving lies

Bridge:

Shame we couldn't work it out
When you decided not to come round anymore
And now I know exactly what for
But even when it came to this end
There was no reason why we couldn't stay friends for life
It would have been alright.

Love Rain Down

2nd Oct 98

Chorus:

Love rain down
On me now
Fill my heart
With joy and hope
Send my spirit
Into the sky
Because I know that there's a way
And I know I'll see the light some day

V1:

Life sometimes can be very lonely
You can feel like you're going it alone
But are you ever really on your own?
Not if you have love in your heart
To guide you through the dark
I know sometimes friends can be cold
But you must hold on
And allow love to make you strong
You'll never fall

V2:

Sometimes people don't understand
That you're only human
And feelings can get hurt
But without the hurt
How will you ever learn
To stand up for yourself
When you do need some help
You know where you can turn to
Because there'll always be enough of love

Bridge:

In your time of need
Please do not retreat
Stand up on your feet and walk tall
Please trust your dream
To show you the way
Don't ever fall.
Follow your dream
I know that it seems hard
But don't ever
Let down your guard
I know you'll find a way
And I know you'll get there soon, one day.

Sometimes

1st Nov '98

Chorus:

Sometimes
Sometimes you need to
Be alone
Be on your own
But sometimes
Sometimes you need to know
Your friends are there
And they'll always care
For you
It's all about you

V1:

Don't you get too isolated
I've been worrying 'bout you for sometime
I won't ever leave you brother
Cos you're a real good friend of mine
You've locked yourself away from me
Wish I could get into your mind
Cos you've got so much of life to live
And I want to see you fly

V2:

I've been trying very hard
To see just what the problem is
I know you want to be alone
But there's so much you've already missed
Lord knows I've tried to help you out
But you're still caught in the rain
Yes I've heard you scream and shout
But I don't want you to give in to the strain
I don't want to see you fade away

Bridge:

It's all about you
You
It's your life that you're missing
It's all about you
You
I want you to get through the rain
But please
Understand what I mean
Understand when I say
That you can't keep living this way
But please
Let me help you sometimes
I want you to see the sun shine again
But I know that

Sometimes
Sometimes you need to
Be alone
Be on your own
But sometimes
Sometimes you need to know
Your friends are there
And they'll always care
For you
It's all about you

No Longer A Slave

1st Nov 98

Chorus:

I am no longer a slave
You showed me through all the rain
I believed I would get there one day
Then you made my dream come true
Because I believed in you

V1:

Not long ago
I was a slave
Trapped inside a lie
But oh my dear Lord
Then you came
And freed me from inside
Cos I knew when I prayed
To you every night
After the fight
That I had from within
Soon love would stay
And not disappear
And I would see clear again

V2:

A long time ago
I went astray
But then you found me
And began to show me the way
Oh Lord you set me free
After the nights when I prayed
Like a shepherds lamb you guided me
As we strolled together through the rain

Bridge:

Oh Lord
You blessed me so amazingly
Like a bird that's free
I fly
Oh Lord
When I needed you so desperately
You came to me
From inside

Whisper Away

2nd Nov

Chorus:

I tell myself that you're only a whisper away
I can't believe you've gone from me
But I knew it had to be some day
You're a whisper away

V1:

Every time I think about it
I can't believe it's true
You always used to care for me
But now it's too late to care for you
Every night I pray that you
Went up to the sky okay
And I tell myself that I
Will see your face again some day

V2:

You lived a long and fulfilled life
But I kept myself in denial
And now come all the questions why
Did you allow yourself to die
You went from me so suddenly
And in such a tragic way
But I keep asking myself
Why could you not stay

Bridge:

Every night I pray
That you found your way
Up into heaven
Inside of me I cry
Keep asking myself why
But I hope that you're happy
Because I
Never said goodbye
When you were lying still
Was the only time I tried
To tell you that I
That I did need you
That I
That I will love you
Always
But you're only a whisper away

Saturday Night

3rd Nov

Chorus:

Saturday
Saturday's the night
When I feel alright
Because I'll see your face again
I can picture it in black and white
When I hold you tight again
Every Saturday night

V1:

After a hard day's night
I finally turn off the light
Finally escape the hurt
That I feel inside
I lay down on my pillow
And close my eyes
And I can finally rest my body
Until the sun does rise

V2:

Gotta go off to work again
Although it's Saturday
I need a rest
But I know that soon
I'll see your face
Greet your presence with a warm embrace
And I know my heart will change its pace
Because tonight's the night again

Bridge:

Sunday
Monday
Tuesday nights
Are not the same
Wednesday
Thursday
Friday nights
I'm still in the rain
But Saturday night
Is the one night
That I'm with you
All night through
And I feel fine
Every Saturday night

Where Am I?

Chorus:

Where am I?
Somewhere I do believe
Somewhere inside of me
I'm sure
But I can't find the open door
Where am I?
Somewhere where I will see
There is much more to me
If I believe
But right now I need to find the key

V1:

Quiet silence
Nothing is disturbed
Tired of waiting
So long it feels absurd
Days of magic
Months of hurt
But along with all the hurt
Inside I learn
To stand on my two feet
To walk and believe
To understand that anything
I can and will achieve

V2:

Sometimes when I'm
All by myself
I often feel like
There is no one else
But I do realise
Some people are there to help
And some people will always be
There for you
In times of need
To care for you
When you are weak
Don't be scared to follow a dream

Where am I?
Somewhere
But I'm not too sure

Finding It So Hard

Chorus:

I'm finding it so hard
To keep going
All of my strength has gone
How long will I have to
Keep on going
On and on and on and on
And on
On and on and on and on
And on
And on

V1:

Here I am
Surrounded in stone
I'm trying to break free
But I feel so alone
The rain is so strong
It sure knows how to hurt
I'm tired of the tears that flow
I'm really sinking in this dirt

V2:

Lord please
I'm waiting for you
To touch my life
I'm getting so tired of waiting
I really need you in my life

I'm finding it so hard
I'm finding it so hard
I'm finding it so hard to go on

I'm finding it so hard
Finding it so hard
Finding it so hard to go on

By My Side

Chorus:

I need you to be
By my side
For all eternity
I need you to
Come home
Because without your love
I'm dying so desperately
And I can't stand being alone
I don't like to be on my own

V1:

Lord knows
When you went away from me
The world stopped spinning
And Lord knows
I'm wanting you so desperately
Cos I can't stand being alone
But you're gone
And you're not coming home to me

V2:

When I
First received the bad news
My head hurt
I became so confused
But now I'm finally
Getting my head around it
But I still don't understand
Why you went ahead with your plan

Bridge:

You went away from me
So suddenly
So tragically
You just passed away
You went away from me
And I never said goodbye
Never found out why
I should have said goodbye

I Am Worth It

16th Nov

Chorus:

I am worth every penny
I receive
I am worth all the love
You give to me
I am worth watching the sun set
In the deep blue sea
I am worth it
I am worth it

V1:

The Lord God does love me
And he will make me be
Because I am worth it
Yeah I am worth it
I stare up at the moon
To push away my gloom
Because I'm worth it
Yeah I am worth it

V2:

Every night I wish on a star
And I believe my wish will go far
Because I am worth it
Yeah I am worth it
I often question 'do I deserve all this love?'
Cos you come to me with more than enough
But I am worth it
Yeah I am worth it

Bridge:

Everyone is worth
More than they own
So don't throw your life away
Everyone can
Still make it big
Just be a kid at heart
You'll find it's the best way to start
Because you're worth it
Yeah you're worth it

Lord Please Forgive Me

Chorus:

Lord please forgive me
Forgive me for all that I have done
I know that I'm not the only one
But sometimes I can feel like I am
Lord please forgive me
Forgive me for all the sins I've made
I know it's not too late
To repent
And try again

V1:

Sometimes I know I can act so selfishly
Feel that there's no one else but me
But I know that I care
And sometimes I can accept things so ungratefully
When there are so many others out there
Who may be needing me to care for them
When they're feeling weak
When they feel life is not worth living
And feel so incomplete

V2:

My life used to be 'not happening'
Felt like everyone was looking in
But I could not see outside
But then my life changed so dramatically
Cos I learned that you were there for me
And would make things alright
But how do I repay you
For all the love you've given me
And Lord how do I show you
That I do believe?

Bridge:

There are so many people out there
Who live their lives without care
Of others
Why do we keep on fighting so much
How did we ever lose all our love
We're sisters and brothers
Can't we love one another

Little Precious

3rd Dec

Chorus:

You used to call me
Your 'little precious'
You said I would be
From now till forever
But now you're gone
Does that still go on
Inside?
And when you left
Without a reason
It hurt so hard
It felt much like treason
You were the only one
I really let inside
And I just can't say goodbye

V1:

When you both went away from me
I was almost sixteen
But back then it didn't really sink in
Cos I found it hard to believe
How could you have disappeared over night
You just went away, right out of sight
But not out of mind
You soared to the sky
Left a letter inside the house
And you'll never be coming round

V2:

You always used to look after me
During my younger years
But now you're gone and I'm in disbelief
Trying to hold back the tears
But I know I can't hold them back for years
I'm well aware
Trying to believe that you're gone
Finding the strength to go on
It's so hard
It's such a long process
And there's so much
I've barely scratched off the surface
But I'm finding my strength inside
And somehow I know I'll get by

Bridge:

I've had some time to think it through
Though life just won't be the same without you by my side
Oh Lord knows I loved you
Lord knows I cared
Lord knows I would do anything to bring you back to me
But that won't ever be
How do you bring someone back from the afterlife
There's no way
You had your life
And went away
And Lord knows I pray
To him every night
Please make sure
That you're alright
Cos I can't say goodbye
I just can't say goodbye

One More Chance

Chorus:

Oh Lord
Please give me one more chance
I know that I will pass
If you just give me more time
Oh Lord
Please hear me when I pray
Make my badness go away
I want to leave it all behind

V1:

Oh Lord
I try so very hard
But I keep letting down my guard
And then the badness comes back
Please Lord
Forgive me of my sin
I know that I can win
If you just give me your hand
I try and try and try
But only you know why I get to nowhere
Life's never felt so tough
But I refuse to give up, somehow I'll get there
If you just give me more time

V2:

Dear Lord
I am sticking to it
I know somehow I'll get through it
At the end of the day
Good Lord
Only you can help me
Lord I seek your safety
I know there's got to be a way
I beg and beg and beg
Please make true what you said to me
Cos Lord I can't go on
How long till I can live in harmony
Please just give me more time

Bridge:

Please can you just trust me
I want to show the world
Exactly who I am
Oh please reach out to me
My dream must come true
Exactly how we planned
Oh Lord
I can do good
As well as bad
Please just give me your hand

Long Lost Love

12th Dec

Chorus:

Love
My long lost love
You are all I need
And you will always be
With me
For all eternity
Love me
For all of time to come
You will be the only one

V1:

Have I seen you?
Maybe once or twice
Have I met you?
Only in my dreams
But I can't forget you
When you whisper tenderly
That you'll always be there for me
Forever and forever
I've never touched you
Never touched your face
But I'll be with you
Forever in this place
Forever in this heart
You'll never go away
You'll be right here to stay
You will always be with me

V2:

You reach out gently
Gentle as the wind
And as you hold me
I don't want this moment to end
You keep me safely
Wrapped up in your arms
And touch me softly
No threat, all is calm
You'll always protect me
From all of life's harms
You'll always love me
Forgive all the bad I've done
And I'll melt so sweetly
As you work your charm
Always in my heart
Always
You'll always be a part
Of me

Bridge:

So when my heart's broken
You will make it mend
So when I start something
I know I'll see it through to the end
Because you are my bestest friend
So when I'm going somewhere
I'm never there alone
And when I'm going nowhere
I'll know I'm never on my own
And it will always be this way till the end
Because you are my bestest friend

Untitled

Chorus:

Lord I love you
Please make it be soon
Lord I trust you
To make your word come true
I'll never leave you
And that much you know
Lord I believe in you
And I always will

V1:

Lord knows how many times
I've asked you to forgive me of my sin
And Lord knows I try to repent
Again and again and again
Lord knows I've made enough sins
Deep enough to swim in
But knows that I can do good
And someday soon I'll win
This battle inside myself
With no one else but me
And Lord knows I'll be beside myself
When this battle is won and I'm free

V2:

Lord knows how many times
I've asked you to please make it be now
And Lord knows how many times
I've told you I can't live without
And Lord knows just how many times
I've cried to you out loud
And Lord, you know that soon it will be
And I'll be singing to that crowd
That beat me up
Psychologically
When my defenses were down
And only you were there for me

Bridge:

Trust me to keep it real
Let me show them the deal
Love me and I'll make it right
I'll show them the light of day
Because once found
You'll never go away

Star Shining Bright

13th Dec

Chorus:

Star shining bright
Guide me with your light
Take me to my savior Jesus Christ
Light up the night
Let your light shine
Let everyone see the one who will change their life
Let everyone see the one at Christmas time

V1:

He was born
Many years ago
But his story lives on
And makes our spirits grow
Now he's sung in a song
That makes us feel alright
And it will always be this way
Until the end of time

V2:

He planted his seed
Deep inside our hearts
And he fills us with peace
And we'll never grow apart
He's somewhere inside
Every one of us
He fills us with pride
And lets us know we're loved

V3:

We're proud to know him
All our lives
He'll always teach us
Make our spirits wise
We won't forget him
Although people say
Cos Jesus Christ our savior
Was born on Christmas Day

Christmas Just Won't Be The Same

14th Dec

Chorus:

Christmas
Christmas
Just won't be the same without you by my side
Without you in my life
Christmas
When I open my presents I'll get no surprise
Although I'll try
You'll still be gone

V1:

Won't get up early on Christmas morning
Won't wait for Santa on Christmas Eve
Won't enjoy buying the presents
Won't help decorate the tree
Won't sing carols at the church
Cos I'm just in too much hurt to be
Away from you
You should be with me
Won't let Santa fill my stocking
When I hear laughter
I feel that they're mocking me
My mind just aint right
There is so much hurt inside of me

V2:

Tried to get into the Christmas spirit
Tried so hard but it just won't work
I'm not in the mood for giving
Since you've gone my minds a blur
I've watched the snow fall outside
But it still doesn't bring you back to life for me
My Christmas just won't be complete
People outside snowball fighting
But I'm just in the mood for crying
Already done a lot of sighing
But that won't bring you back to me

Bridge:

I just don't feel alive
Lord please tell me why
I would rather sit and cry
Than have a load of fun outside
I won't help to feed the poor
Give them more then they asked for
But nothing would surprise me more
Than to have you standing at my door

I'm Going To See It Through

Chorus:

I'm going to see it through
So long as you're by my side
I'm going to see it through
See the sun rise
I've got nothing else to lose
I've lost nearly everything that ever really mattered to me
Lord won't you make my dream
Make my dream reality

V1:

I'm ashamed to admit it
But I'm a little scared
I thought that after all this time
I would have been properly prepared
I'm nervous
My hands are shaking as I write this down tonight
When your dreams about to come true
You'd think I'd be feeling fine
But I'm breaking out in a sweat
Thoughts rushing through my head
What if it don't turn out right?
My heads pounding
I can feel every move it makes
A small part of me wants to stay the same
Don't know why
But it's there
And a part of me doesn't mind
But Lord I know what I want
Don't get me wrong
I know what I want inside

V2:

Still nervous
I had a bath but that didn't work
Still shaking
Tried to relax
Think of things I'd like most
But what I would like most of all
Is to have you standing by me tall
Telling me it's nearly complete
These nerves
They feel like the ones you get
Before you go on stage
Though I've yet to make my way down that lane
I don't want things to stay the same
I want everything to change right now
Somehow
Please don't get me wrong
But I don't like what I've got from you
People say 'be happy with what you got'
'Be proud'
So is my way of thinking
One that's not allowed?
Still…

Bridge:

My nerves
I think they're getting the best of me
I'm finding it hard to see
Though I believe
In you
And what people say you've done
I know that I wait for much
But you said this must be done…

No Looking Back

25th Dec 98

Chorus:

No looking back
That's one thing I refuse to do
I know that I will see it through
No looking back.
No looking back
Cos when I do there's only tears
I know I've got to break through here
No looking back
No looking back

V1:

If I do look back
To before this hurt began
It makes me oh so sad
But I
Have come a long way now
And I refuse
To turn back around
My feet are on the ground
But my head's to the sky
Because I believe in time
Time heals
Everything that's going wrong
Time heals
Never stops, it carries on
Time heals everything in time
Keep your fingers crossed that faith is on your side

V2:

When I
Do look forward
It keeps
It keeps me going strong
It's all I'm living on
My dream
I know I'll see it through
My dream
I've got nothing else to lose
My dream
It will become real
It's what I feel
Deep inside my heart
It's what I feel
And it won't grow apart
It's in my heart
For all time
And time and love, they work side by side

Time heals
Everything that's going wrong
Times heals
Never stops, it carries on
Time heals everything in time
Keep your fingers crossed that change is on your side
It's what I feel
Deep inside my heart
It's what I feel
And it won't grow apart
It's in my heart
For all of time
And time and love
They work side by side

Poem

'99

All day long
The boy sings his song
Night and day
Until he lays
And breathes a sigh of relief
As his song takes him away from his grief
'Could have beens' he thinks of not
But 'One day will be's' are in his thoughts
He was not taught to sing his song
He thought of it himself
For when he sings
Of beautiful things
He takes himself away from hell
Why should he ponder on bad things
That take the light of day
When he has so much to look forward to
He will get there soon
One day

Poem

Run little children
Be as free as can be
Don't be infected
By adolescence or puberty
Don't grow up
Don't grow old
Let innocence
Take control

Run little children
Into a fantasy world
Where rules aren't there to be broken
And where adults aren't heard
Be as innocent
As that little white bird
Bring power to your voice
Make sure it is heard

Run little children
Straight into bed
Don't stay up late
Don't be misled
By all the violence
And evil desires
Don't let it all
Get into your head

Run little children
Run little children

Poem

Where am I
Somewhere
I'm not too sure
I could be on the moon
Or behind four walls
I am not quite sure
If I am ready for this change
But I know one thing
Life cannot stay the same

I Need Reassurance

22nd March '99

V1:

I need to talk
With you Lord
I don't know what else there is that I can do
I've tried nearly everything
That I can think of
But so far my situations not improved at all
Lord please tell me what you want from me
So I can serve
And then begin to fulfill my destiny

Chorus:

I need your help
To follow my dream
Please let me know
What the future holds for me
I can't go on
Without reassurance.
I need reassurance

V2:

Can you hear
What I'm saying
How long until you answer all my praying?
I've been waiting so long
But I won't ever stop believing in you
My love
Should grow stronger for you every day
But instead
It just seems to remain the same
I'm so sorry

Bridge:

My love for you
Just seems to remain the same
But I know my love for you
Will never fade
I just need reassurance

Untitled [later called 'I Refuse']

14th April 99

(The day I was told I was being discharged in 2 days' time)

Chorus:

I refuse to accept what you want me to
I refuse to accept because it ain't right
When I've been here for so long
I'm trying to figure out what's wrong
Yet you expect me to be able to say goodbye
I think you're out of your mind

V1:

I have been here
For over half a year
Are you saying I've wasted my time?
I have kept it cool
Obeyed all of the rules
But now it turns out that you were the ones who lied
Don't you feel ashamed?
Don't you feel disgraced?
Knowing that I'm in the right
But you feel the need
To keep things away from me
And you know that, you cannot deny

V2:

We had a deal
Could you not keep it real?
I can't believe that I was so blind
You lied from the start
Told me I would get far
You really tried to pull the wool over my eyes
Don't you feel ashamed?
Don't you feel disgraced?
Knowing that I'm in the right
But you feel the need
To keep things away from me
And you know that, you cannot deny

Bridge:

This song has no name
But it's written in a lot of pain
Pain that came from you
You're practically saying that it's tough
But I've about had enough
Somehow I know I've got to get through
Because I refuse.

Allowed To Feel Down

22nd April 99

Chorus:

I'm allowed
To feel down if I want to
Don't blame me
If there's nothing that I want to do
I know that
I'll snap out of it real soon
But right now
Let me be alone
I need to sort some stuff out on my own

V1:

I need some time to think
About what's happening to me
Right now my life just seems
To be full of misery
I don't understand what I've done
To feel all this pain
I know that I'll pick myself up
But not today

V2:

I know that you are worried
Thanks for coming around
But I don't need any of your help
At least not right now
I appreciate that you want
To try to do your best
But it's not really any
Of your business

Bridge:

I can see the sun shining
After the rain
And I know that tomorrow
Is the start of a new day
Let's just see how I go
If I feel better I shall let you know
But right now I just want
To be left alone

Can you please go
Cos you should know
We all need to be alone
Every now and then

It Happens Every Day
(In response to Jill Dando's murder)

26th April

V1:

It started out as just an ordinary day
Everything around me had remained the same
But then out of the blue
Came the tragic news
Someone had been found
Lying still on the ground
Everyone around me was in disbelief
How could someone like that be killed so tragically
Someone in the public eye
Now taken out of our sight
How could this happen
To someone so innocent?

Chorus:

It happens every day
But does that make it ok?
No way
There's no place for this hate
Things cannot stay the same
Somehow we've got to make a change
Cos these people
They're insane
Killing others to them is just a game

V2:

Now it's not every day someone well known gets killed
But you can guarantee that someone else still will
Be murdered in some way
By people fuelled with hate
Whose reason holds a grudge
On someone else's love
Well they need to be locked up with keys thrown away
Where they're no longer a threat to the human race
But some people still get away
Even when they've cause so much heartache
Some get out in a few years
Once again causing much fear

Bridge:

I'm sure that in most cases
Authorities do the best they can
But they cannot bring back
What was taken by fellow man
Can we not destroy weapons
And try to live in peace
Everyone I know
Does not want this insanity

If you do know something
Tell the authorities
Cos if you keep it to yourself
You'll never live peacefully

Dream Of Me Tonight

14th May

Chorus:

Could you please
Dream of me
Tonight
Imagine that
I'm right by
Your side
Cos every night
Although I try
I can't get you out of my mind
So could you please
At least try to think of me
Tonight

V1:

Where are you
I need you
I need someone to talk to
I miss you
I need you in my life
I can't help
But think of
That something we let go of
It just won't
Escape my mind.
Every time
I lay me down
I can't help but wonder
Where you are now
I know it sounds weak
But right now I'm in need
Of you
Could you spare a thought for me

V2:

I feel so
Lonely
I miss my one and only
But do you
Realise that that's you
I have reason
To doubt that
Because I never said that
I never
Could tell you the truth.
Just before
I fall asleep
I hope I see
You in my dreams
I know it sounds weak
But right now I'm in need
Of you
Could you spare a thought for me

Bridge:

If you're not in my life
You're still in my mind
And I'm not letting go
Because I want another try
I have realised
That I may have been blind
But I want you to know
That I'm thinking of you tonight

Poem

Are you thinking of me
Like I'm thinking of you
Am I on your mind every day
Are you missing me
Like I'm missing you
I'm wondering if we're feeling the same
You never got to know me
For who I really am
But now I want to show you
If you'd only understand
I want to be back in your company
I want to be there
Whenever you need me
I know it hasn't been long
But it feels like eternity
I want you back with me
I miss your company.

Poem

Why does nothing ever
Come easy
You open up your heart
For no reason
Yes some people care
But there are so many liars out there
Who only think about themselves
And don't care about anyone else
So long as they have their wealth
They don't care about your health
But some people truly care
And I am one of them
And I know some of them

One Day Closer

Chorus:

Every day is one day closer to heaven
I know eventually I will get there
If I believe and have faith
He will show me the way
Therefore I know that with every passing day
I'm one day closer to heaven

V1:

Sometimes it seems
I've come so far but got nowhere
But still I keep going on
People come and go
Leaving me in the cold dark lonely night
That is life
I keep on going
Although I feel weak
Never quite knowing
If I'll find what I seek
It seems this journey
Is never ending for me
But every day I get up
And I keep working hard
Because I won't give in
And I'll keep looking at the stars
And I know that with every day
With every passing day
I'm closer

V2:

The road is long
And I don't know how much of it is left
I can't see too clearly ahead
But if I look back
I've travelled too far to change my mind
No point in returning
To what I left behind
I've been cut and I've been scarred
But even so I've come this far
And I ain't gonna turn around
Because I'm not one to back down

Bridge:

It may only be one day less
And I don't know how many are left
But I know if I believe
And keep dreaming my dream
I will get there
I will get there

Poem

I know how it feels
At least I know what it feels like to me
People just don't understand
That you haven't got what you need
I know it's hard to keep going
In a world where you feel you don't fit in
But you've got a chance to prove everyone else wrong
So you're going to keep going
And you're not going to give in
Don't listen to what all the other people say
If you believe then you're already on your way
Just look at other people for proof
There ain't nothing you can't do

Poem

I've had it up to here
With unnecessary fear
My mind is never clear
There's just too much going on
But nobody else sees
What's happening to me
I can't give in to defeat
Therefore I have to be strong
I have love for everybody
But I feel nobody loves me
I don't know if this is true
Or just low self esteem
I know I love my creator
But does he love me
He hasn't shown it yet
But the Bible says wait patiently
So I'll wait as patiently as I can
Though that will be hard for me to do
Cos I'm an agitated man
Who right now feels he has no use
I have so many plans
Which have yet to come true
My father won't you tell me
What else there is that I must do

Tom Clement

Poem

Please make no promises to me
You let me down on everything.

Nothing Left To Give

6th June '99

Chorus:

You have taken everything
And now there's nothing left to give
All I wanted was your love
All that's left is emptiness
Can't we try to work things out
Cos I just cannot live like this
Don't know why you feel you should receive
When you give nothing back to me

V1:

Don't mean to be rude
But you can't expect it your way all the time
You just come round when you choose
You know that that ain't right
You know I have true love for you
But that don't mean you can do whatever you feel
You go, then come back round
Pretending everything's fine
What's the deal
I can't go on living this way
You can stay
But this situation's got to change

V2:

All I'm asking for
Is for me to see love come from you
But still you seem to ignore
Everything I say or do
Loving you feels like a chore
But when I've finished, what have I gained
I've always loved you
And I don't want to throw my love away
I can't go on living this way
You can stay
But this situation's got to change

Bridge:

Don't know what you expect from me
When I have nothing left to give
I just can't stop loving you
Though you don't keep your promises

Poem

I'll just sleep and be sad and be lonely
Let the day just pass me by
And I'll tuck my head under my duvet
Maybe then I'll be alright
If I sleep then I'll dream and I'll be far away
From all this hurt inside
Even my dream isn't reality
Just a place in my mind.
Dreaming is what keeps me alive.

Come To Me

Chorus:

Come to me
You're the one I need
Without you I can't breathe
I'm so lonely
And when you come to me
Don't you ever leave me
Alone

V1:

Too depressed
To cry
No energy
Left inside
Feeling numb
All throughout
Only you
Can make the cloud
Above my head
Disappear
I want you
I need you right here

V2:

Feeling sad
Head hung low
Can't explain
All this hurt
Feeling cold
So alone
The intensity
Of this misery

My Dove

22nd Oct '99

Chorus:

Where is my dove
My symbol of peace
Where is my love
The one that I need
I'll give you my white flag
But only if it means
That after you celebrate the success of your petty ways
You'll leave us in peace

V1:

I know we've spent a lot of our time fighting
For no other reason than to really hurt each other
I know we've spent a lot of our time crying
When there's already so much unnecessary pain in this world
There are people living without lives
Some people are so uncaring that they blow out other peoples
lights
They think it's funny to make others lose their spark for life
When good people end up going dry
When all their emotions been drained from them
And all their love has been numbed by mistrust
If a price can never be put on a life
Then how come so many are lost over night

V2:

When you hear the voice of someone speaking the truth
It goes through your ear, realises there's no brain, and comes out
of your eye
Then you immediately shout out a load of feeble excuses
Trying to make people believe that you're in the right
How can you truly justify what you do
When you know there's no way on earth that you'll ever be able to
You don't even admit the truth
You just lie away to yourself thinking they'll never find proof
Well what makes you think you have the right
To effect so many people's lives
How can you be unable to see
That your actions effect so many

Bridge:

Somebody kills somebody
Then his friends get revenge
Then friends get their revenge for the revenge
Then friends get their revenge for the revenge of the revenge
How will this dangerous cycle ever end

Open the cage
Let the dove fly away
Let it be free
Let it bring peace.

Some Songs Unfinished

When you fall asleep
Babe that's when I'll be
As far away from you as I can be
What we had was tough
Couldn't really call it love
I'm tired of the times that you hurt me...

Change For The Better

V1:

I know you've had some hard times
I know you've had a hard life
But you've got to know things will
Change for the better
I know some people ain't nice
They've really tried to screw up your life
But you know you can make things
Change for the better

Chorus:

Things are going to change for the better
I know that you're feeling under the weather
But things will happen soon, sooner or later
You've got to realise you, you have the power

Evolution

V1:

I was once a small child
I dreamed about the world
And I knew that I'd find my place
And throughout the hard times
I kept my dream alive
It was something I'd dare not erase
And when the times were hard
And when the nights were cold
I locked my dream inside my heart
And left it there to grow

Chorus:

We came from nowhere
But look what we've gained
Evolution
The process of change.

I haven't looked at these lyrics for ten years. They were too entwined with my time in the hospital and the painful months that came after. Also I didn't believe that I was 'ill' then, but in the time that's passed it's been hammered in to me that I was 'ill' then, and I came to think of these lyrics as irrelevant to now and showing the mind of a crazy person.

In writing and remembering these lyrics for this book. I remember how I felt writing some of these songs. I felt I knew who I was, and I was my own person. Before my certainty of who I am crumbled. When writing these up, I've realized that I was sure of myself before the way of the psychiatric system crawled under my skin. Professionals in the psychiatric field don't allow you to just ' be '. They constantly question you and want you to question yourself. They want you to question everything you think, say and do. You can't just make a decision, without it having to be broken down. Being exposed to too much of this makes a person start to question themselves and makes them have to analyse their beliefs, like the professionals do, until they don't know what to believe, or who they are anymore. That's what's happened to me.

Reading these lyrics back, I don't think they are the words of a crazy person. They're the works of a young soul trying to express his hopes and frustrations about the environment he was living in. And reading them back, some seem more relevant to now than ever. I've never shown them to anyone before. And I'm glad I've finally felt able to share them here.

Tom Clement.

My obligatory author pic ☺

And my bestest buddy bunny boy, Riot ☺

Some important websites for mental health:

Time To Change www.time-to-change.org.uk

A combined positive movement by the UK's leading mental health charities to break down the stigma and discrimination that excists around mental health illnesses.

Black Dog Tribe www.blackdogtribe.com

A friendly community for people who've experienced mental distress

Mind www.mind.org.uk

An amazing resource point for information on mental illness

I would rather be mindless, than heartless

T.Clement

www.ingramcontent.com/pod-product-compliance
Lightning Source LLC
Chambersburg PA
CBHW031213270326
41931CB00006B/550